Nemai Ghosh is best known ...
Satyajit Ray and his stills from Ray's films. He has
exhibited at Cannes in 1991, at London in 1992,
and several times at Calcutta and Delhi. Ghosh
began his artistic career as an actor. He is the
author of *Faces of Indian Art: Through the Lens of Nemai
Ghosh*, *Satyajit Ray: A Vision of Cinema* (with Andrew
Robinson), *Satyajit Ray at 70*, among others.

S.K. Ray Chaudhuri worked as a geologist with
Cement Corporation of India and other public and
private sector organizations till 2001. He then took
to freelancing as a geological consultant and also as
an editor with leading publishing houses in India.
His translation of a biography of S.D. Burman is
forthcoming.

MANIK-DA

Memories of Satyajit Ray

NEMAI GHOSH

Translated by
S.K. Ray Chaudhuri

HarperCollins *Publishers* India

First published in Bengali in 2000 by Bingsha Shatabdi, Kolkata
First published in French in 2001 by Bingsha Shatabdi, Kolkata
This edition published in India in 2011 by
HarperCollins *Publishers* India
Building No 10, Tower A, 4th Floor, DLF Cyber City, Phase II,
Gurugram – 122002
www.harpercollins.co.in

1 2 3 4 5 6 7 8 9 10

Text Copyright © Nemai Ghosh 2011

P-ISBN: 978-93-5029-040-8
E-ISBN: 978-93-5029-953-1

Nemai Ghosh asserts the moral right
to be identified as the author of this work

Typeset in Weiss 11/15.7

To my wife, Sibani

Contents

A Note from the Bengali Publisher

Bengalis are a sentimental people. They brim with emotion just as easily as they distance themselves from it.

As an example one may cite the case of a film-maker in the 1930s, Pramathesh Chandra Barua. He was a pioneer who raised the standard of Indian films from just a stagecraft to that of the very distinct art of the motion picture. If it had not been for his contribution, Bengali, for that matter even Indian cinema would not have been what it is today. However, many of Bengal's so-called culture czars have not even heard of him or do not remember him.

A lot has been said and written about Satyajit Ray. Many papers have been published on him and his work both in India and abroad. This book is yet another attempt to understand and appreciate the genius that was Satyajit Ray, the man who brought Bengali cinema to the world stage.

Books on him that have been published abroad are beyond the reach of the ordinary Bengali reader. Keeping this in mind, this book has been priced so that it is accessible to the ordinary reader, without compromising on quality.

The author of this book, Nemai Ghosh, had a long-standing association with Ray, one that makes him a witness of his personal as well as working life. Ray has been immortalized in his camera. This book aims to share with its readers some unknown facets of the legendary film-maker, keeping his memory alive in the form of some rare and insightful photographs.

Maitrali Mukhopadhyay

Calcutta Book Fair, 2000

Author's Note

During a recent session of our usual adda, Kanchana Mukhopadhyay was present while I was narrating how I switched over to photography from theatre, my first love, by virtue of being close to Manik-da. Thinking of the future generation she brought up a proposal to publish, on behalf of Bingsha Shatabdi, an album in Bengali containing some photographs and some reminiscences. Without any hesitation, I concurred immediately. I am sincerely grateful to her and to the publisher.

I have received help in many ways in preparing this album from Gautam Sengupta, Bikash Basu,

Sanjay Sau, Ranjini Chattopadhyay, Soumik Nandi Majumdar, and Satyaki Ghosh. The christening is by Rituparna Ghosh. I am grateful to all of them.

I express my gratitude to my friend Shiladitya Sen who has unflinchingly helped in the process of shaping this book.

I am grateful to HarperCollins *Publishers* India for bringing out the book in English. I hope my humble effort reaches a wider readership through this endeavour.

Foreword

Sharmila Tagore

I have known Nemai Ghosh for a long time now. If you ask me to be precise about where and how we met, I haven't the foggiest idea, but it feels like I have known him forever. What we had in common was Manik-da, who happened to be a mentor to both of us. Till such time that he met Manik-da, incredulous as it may sound, he had no knowledge of professional photography. Despite that, Manik-da decreed that Nemai Ghosh would be the official stills photographer for *Aranyer Dinratri*. Naturally, like many others, I too had my doubts, but of course no one dared oppose Manik-da. And once again how right Manik-da was and how wrong we were! As they say, the proof of the pudding is in eating, and the stills of *Aranyer Dinratri* were proof enough of the man's sheer genius. What a perfect backdrop it was to begin with – the magical forest of Palamau, with its skeletal trees, must have been the perfect inspiration. Not that Simi, Kaveri-di or I were bad subjects either, not to mention Soumitra Chatterjee, Robi-da, Shubhendu, Samit, and last but not the least, the photogenic Manik-da.

Thus began our lifelong association. He has immortalized Manik-da in iconic poses which will remain with us forever. And anybody who knew Manik-da well would know how closely Nemai-da's photographs reflect his persona. As I called him in another context, he was indeed the visual Boswell to Ray's Johnson.

And yet, Nemai-da is not only about Ray. Given his natural retiring disposition, not many people know that he was quite a stalwart of Bengali theatre in the 1950s and 1960s. After his career-altering meeting with Ray, he gradually moved away from active theatre. But he used his new-found passion to document the world of Bengali theatre in *Dramatic Moments*, a brilliant book replete with breathtaking images. He has also documented the world of Indian art in *Faces of Indian Art: Through the Lens of Nemai Ghosh*. More recently, he collaborated with celebrated artist Paresh Maity on a book of photographs and paintings, *The World on a Canvas*, for which I wrote the text. What sets his art apart is the fact that he shoots only in natural light and has never ever used the flash or artificial lighting. Also, even in this era he shoots primarily in black and white.

It gives me great pleasure to write the Foreword to this book. Its Bengali edition has been a great success and it also has a French edition. It is only right that Indian readers should know about the close association between India's greatest film-maker and his photographer as they scripted visual history. Thanks to this translation, that is now possible. Much like the relationship between Manik-da and Nemai-da, the text is warm and intimate, without being extravagant or flashy. The brilliant, so far unpublished photographs, give

an insight into the easy camaraderie that existed
between the two. I am sure this will be an invaluable
addition to film literature in the country.

Manik-Da

The word 'cinema' has now become inextricably entwined with my name. Any talk about me invariably leads to photography. But surprisingly, I was never supposed to be a photographer at all.

Though it may sound unbelievable, it is a fact that right since childhood my dreams were centred only around drama. I started acting in school and later in Utpal Dutt's Little Theatre Group. I acted in their famous play *Angar* and also in *Ferari Fauj*, *Othello*, *Nicher Mahal*, etc. I also played an important role in a play called *Thug* directed by Robi-da (Ghosh).

Theatre left a deep impression on my mind. It helped me later in life in choosing the right settings from behind the camera.

Another lesson from that time was the use of light in photography. The legendary Tapas-da (Sen) used to do the lighting with us in those days. The waxing and waning of the intensity of light had such an effect on me that even today I do not use flash while taking a shot – I just cannot do it. I feel, flash destroys the natural drama of light and darkness.

In fact, my early experience in theatre and my association with Manik-da in later life have prevented me from making any sort of compromise with my work. Manik-da was a perfectionist. If the setting so required, he would visit Nepal to compose two lines of a song; the next two lines would be tuned in some jungle and the next two, on a beach in Chennai.

I must admit, the camera is no longer something outside my existence, distinct from me; it is a part of my person. Just like the sensory organs, I can see many things better with my eye behind the lens.

Bishop Lefroy Road, Kolkata (undated)

For instance, while visualizing the movement of light across a stage with thirty to forty actors in a play is difficult, but when my eye is behind the camera, it becomes clear to me.

Certain episodes reshaped my life and changed its course entirely. I know not who makes such incidents happen. But whosoever he might be, I am eternally grateful to him.

My tryst with the camera is one such episode. Let alone photography, I didn't even know how to click a camera. It was probably 1967 or 1968. A card session was on in full swing in my house. Most of my friends, Shubhendu (Chattopadhyay), Bhanu-da (Ghosh), Bansi (Chandragupta), were associated with films. I was never any good at cards. It was sometime in the afternoon. Snacks were being served – the card game and light refreshment going on together. I stood near the window and was munching some muri (parched rice). I was to leave for rehearsals a little later. I was completely immersed in theatre at that time.

A friend of mine suddenly turned up and said that someone had left behind a fixed-lens camera in a taxi. Another friend of his had already offered him a sum of six hundred rupees for the camera. Something clicked in my mind, and I told him, 'Look, you owe me two hundred forty rupees. You give me the camera and the loan is as good as repaid. Now, you better decide which to choose – business or friendship.'

Sure enough, he left the camera with me. I examined it but could make nothing of it. Realizing my predicament, one of my friends, Jaipratap Mitra, an assistant cameraman, decided to help. Bhanu-da suggested he would arrange for film rolls. Thus, with the help of my friends, in a short span of time, I started viewing everything through the lens of my camera.

My friends and I were in the habit of spontaneous outings. Let me mention here that this habit has never left me, despite advancing age. To tell the truth, I have never devoted much time to any of my three children. But still they have been brought up well. The full credit for this goes to my brothers and my wife Sibani. In fact, we all lived together. And perhaps it is because of the benefits of living in a joint family that I could, and even now can, take such risks. I met Sibani only after our wedding and we have been together for over fifty years now. Meanwhile, I quit my job, stopped acting on stage, spent thousands on film. When fathers of other children escorted them to examination halls, I would perhaps be out on some outdoor shooting or, intoxicated with photography, on the lookout for some other shoot. My wife has never complained about such escapades. Even when I missed many social functions she took responsibility and made excuses for me. She has always demonstrated ample faith in me and my pursuits.

One Saturday, we boarded a train for Barddhaman – the Canon camera and two rolls of film with me. What awaited us there was beyond our wildest dreams. Our host at Barddhaman – a friend of mine – told us that Satyajit Ray was shooting for *Goopy*

Gyne Bagha Byne at nearby Rampurhat. Robi-da, the director of our drama group Chalachal, was playing an important role in the film. I thought, well I could try killing two birds with a stone: see him on the job, and take his photograph also. We were all quite excited!

But having reached there we learnt that the shoot had been cancelled for the day. The unit was busy rehearsing a shot, one that later fascinated film lovers the world over – the shot in which drops of water drip from leaves and fall on Bagha's drum.

I don't know what possessed me then. As if in a trance I felt my finger pressing the shutter on the camera. I finished both rolls of film. We returned to Kolkata the following day.

I went straight to the then famous Studio Renaissance in Ballygunj, owned by Bhupendra Kumar Sanyal, more popularly known as Mej-da. Leading film-makers and creative artists of the time like Satyajit Ray, Mrinal Sen, Ritwik Ghatak, Tapan Sinha and Ravi Shankar used to frequent his studio in those days. Perhaps my association with theatre gave me the courage to go to the studio to

Rampurhat, Birbhum: *Goopy Gyne Bagba Byne*, 1968

develop my films, for there was no reason he would pay any heed to a small fry like me. It transpired that Mr Sanyal had seen me on stage and liked my performance too. That is why I could gather enough courage to hand over the two rolls to him. He took them and with a grave face entered the darkroom.

I waited in eager anticipation, my heart thumping against my ribcage. Each moment seemed like an endless hour. Mej-da was sure to come out and say in his enigmatic voice, 'Well, you were doing fine in theatre. Why then this sudden craze for photography?'

Mej-da came out of the darkroom. The first thing he did was pinch me on the belly and then he kissed my forehead and said, 'Go ahead, you will succeed in photography.'

I couldn't believe my ears. Had I heard it right? This, after just a few days of holding the camera in my hand for the first time. His words still ring in my ears. Praise from such an experienced man in the field gave me a lot of strength and encouragement.

Lake Temple Road, Kolkata: 1968

My excitement knew no bounds. I went on showing those pictures to others. I still vividly remember my joy and surprise at the pleasant response to those photographs. Of course, I did not have the slightest inkling even then as to how the camera would change my life completely.

It was then that Bansi Chandragupta, who used to address Satyajit Ray by his first name, suggested to me that I show Manik-da the photographs.

'Whom?' I asked him in amazement.

He replied, 'Why! Manik, of course. He is shooting for *Goopy Gyne* these days at Tollygunj. Just drop in sometime with these pictures.'

One afternoon a few days later, I dropped by at the studio at Tollygunj, Bansi-da took the packet and said, 'Manik, have a look at these photographs.'

While Manik-da looked at the photographs, I hid behind Bansi-da, nervously watching the six-foot-two-inch man as he attentively went through the photographs shot by an amateur like me. To say I was excited would be an understatement.

He finally spoke. 'Who has taken these photographs?' Bansi-da moved aside, pointed towards me and said, 'This boy, he is Nemai, Nemai Ghosh.' Manik-da looked at me and in his deep baritone said, 'You have done it exactly the way I would have, man, you have got the same angles!'

I was ecstatic! I remember having gooseflesh out of sheer thrill and suspense. Much time has passed since then, but that excitement, I can still feel within me. Even today, when I write about that incident I feel that same excitement so palpably.

Then he himself escorted me to the sets. And that was my initiation.

Soon I found myself in the company of experienced people with modern cameras in hand. It took me a while to get used to the whole ambience. That I could, was perhaps because of the towering personality of Manik-da, which overshadowed everything around him.

Completely overwhelmed by all that I saw around me, I was fascinated by my subject – the magnetic presence of the film-maker as auteur. My lens captured various poses of that intense, self-contained man – the minute trembling of his fingers, the way he sat, walked, the poise with which he stood.

I still held in my hand that Canon fixed-lens camera.

Some members of Manik-da's unit used to meet in the evening at a shop in our neighbourhood. Present at such a gathering, were his art director Bansi Chandragupta, sound recorder Sujit Sarkar, production controller Bhanu Ghosh and many others. They usually discussed the minute details of the day's shooting and also the artistic skills of the film-maker.

In time, I too became a part of the adda. I found myself drawn to it every day on my way back home from my rehearsals. It was like an addiction. However, to begin with, I was only a listener. I wondered when I would know enough to be able to

discuss the nitty gritties of working with Manik-da.
It used to depress me a little, but I would invariably
gravitate to their adda every evening.

In retrospect, I realize that this adda acted
like an inspiration for me. It would remove the
pain of being away from Manik-da. I could feel
his personality radiate through his work and
the various discussions on it. And that was what
kept me going. It gave me a sense of confidence.
Someday, I would also be able, like they were then,
to tell his story.

Meeting Manik-da on the sets was like a dream for
me. But there was a big gap between that dream
and reality.

I was the eldest of my brothers and was married
about ten years prior to my first meeting with
Manik-da. As the head of a joint family, married,
and having children of my own, I had many
responsibilities. I was always worried whether I
would ever be able to devote myself fully to the

fulfilment of my dream. On the one hand, there was my stable, ten-to-five job which would sustain my family, and on the other hand was my first love – theatre.

Even in the face of such harsh realities, I visited Manik-da's set whenever I had spare time. When Bhanu-da told me that Manik-da had framed the photographs I had taken and hung them in his bedroom, I was greatly motivated.

After that first meeting when I showed him my photographs, I met Manik-da again on the sets of *Goopy Gyne*. I was there for about seven or eight shoots. But even within such a short span of time, I saw the man in some of his lonelier moments.

Usually, Manik-da never left the sets during lunchtime. Since I was not a member of the unit, I couldn't accompany the others during breaks. As a result, I studied him from a distance, through my lens.

Once, I saw him standing alone and playing a *dundubhi* (a kettledrum). On another occasion, I saw him lying on the floor and looking at the ceiling; at times I would see him raising his hands above his head in deep contemplation. I noticed that a sign of his deep anxiety or serious contemplation was biting a handkerchief or the pipe. Sometimes, he would whistle a tune, oblivious to the surroundings.

For my photographs of Manik-da which show him laughing heartily, I am deeply indebted to my actor friend Kamu Mukhopadhyay. While I would take different positions – sometimes sitting, sometimes lying, or even standing at precarious angles – Kamu would stand behind me and imitate my pose, making Manik-da break into a loud guffaw.

One morning I came to know that he was leaving for Santiniketan the next day by an early morning train, travelling first class. I bought a third-class ticket and boarded his compartment. He was deeply engrossed in reading a book. I was sure he had not seen me. I clicked away. It was much later

16

that I realized that he had seen everything. When the train halted at a station, he alighted, bought two earthen cups of tea and offered me one.

Manik-da was an early riser. I used to visit him at his place at six-thirty in the morning. In fact, that was the only time he was free and did not have visitors. Later on, of course, there was no fixed time for me to visit his house. His door was always open.

He was always at work. I hardly ever saw him sit idle. Manik-da would get ready by six and come to his drawing room where I would present him with all the contact sheets of my photographs. He would scrutinize these and mark the ones he liked. I still retain those contact sheets. There were occasions when Manik-da would not tick certain photographs that appealed to me. When I asked him, he would explain, like a teacher instructing a student, why those were not good in all respects. Some shots might have been good but the background was not proper. This is how I learnt the art of perfect photography from him.

One thing surprised me then and it strikes me even now. Despite all the name and fame he had attained, he had an uncanny ability to guide any newcomer towards his goal. But he used to get annoyed if someone wanted him to demonstrate how to do something. His mantra was 'do it yourself', though he would act as a guide every step of the way. He would judge a man through his attempts and then guide him in a manner that he could easily follow. In my judgement, he was one of the best actors in the world. I can prove it through my photographs.

After *Goopy Gyne* I again got absorbed in theatre. I was the hero in *Thug* directed by Robi-da. As time passed by in office, rehearsals and shows, whatever had happened over the past few days appeared more like a dream than reality. And with each passing day, cruel reality seemed to overshadow the dream.

But the director of my life's drama had other

plans in mind. One day my telephone rang early in the morning. I lifted the receiver. It was Manik-da. He had called to remind me about his plans for shooting *Aranyer Dinratri*. 'Interesting subject, join if you can,' he said.

I had learnt about *Aranyer Dinratri* a few days ago from our neighbourhood adda. From then on my mind was in Palamau, where the shoot was to happen. And then came his phone call. I would have put on a pair of wings on my back and flown there right away if I could. But hard luck!

Staging *Thug* was imminent and Robi-da was on leave from Chalachal. It was impossible to stage the show in my absence. Besides, I could not explain to anybody how important it was for me to go to Palamau.

So, I stayed back in Kolkata. At the same time, I did not want to miss even a single moment of the shooting. So, in absolute secrecy, I bought a plane ticket, for I had found out that their train and the next day's flight reached at around the same time.

But the plane was delayed due to fog, and on reaching, I learnt that all the buses and cars reserved for the group's journey to Palamau had left. I finally reached the location only by evening. The moment I reached the set, I was told by someone that Manik-da had been looking for me. For the first time I felt important.

Later that evening, Manik-da explained to me the minute details of the shooting and the time the next day's work would commence. Next day, he suddenly told me that I would be responsible for the still photography as he might forget it. I was to take photographs of Manik-da's shooting and that too on his order! It was as if the stars were in my reach! That was the first time I felt I was doing a job which was part of his work.

That single incident boosted my confidence manifold. I felt I could succeed even with my old camera. I simply had to. This self-confidence swept aside all obstacles. Even today I believe that a man who believes in himself and has a genuine desire to succeed in a chosen vocation can surpass any artist skilled and trained in that profession.

I showed my first round of photographs to Manik-da. He marked 'SR' on those he liked and

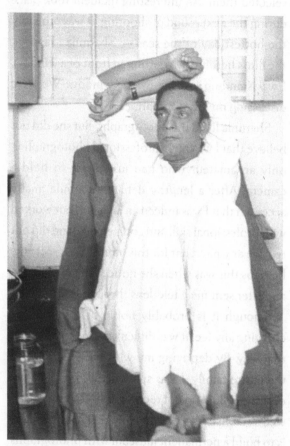

Bishop Lefroy Road, Kolkata, 1969

selected them. An interesting incident took place during the next round of shooting. It was probably the hottest day of the season. Sharmila (Tagore), the film's heroine, was sitting in front of a window. I was standing just below the window. We were discussing my photographs.

Sharmila liked the photographs. But she did not believe that I was not a professional photographer, only an amateur who had just learnt to hold a camera. After a lengthy debate, Sharmila finally accepted that I was indeed an amateur, but worked with professional skill and competence, and did not receive any payment for this, nor did I expect any. Perhaps this was when she noticed my old camera and later sent me a tele-lens through Robi-da.

Though it is probably noble to think of not charging any fee, it was difficult for me to continue that way. By depriving my wife and children and the entire family, I was spending all I had on my obsession. But I do not regret it. My children are all well-established now. The only dream I now have is to build a permanent museum with photographs of Satyajit Ray.

On the bank of the Koel River, Palamau: *Aranyer Dinrati*, 1969

Chipadahar, Palamau: *Aranyer Dinratri*, 1969

Chipadahar, Palamau: *Aranyer Dinratri*, 1969

Chipadahar, Palamau: *Aranyer Dinratri*, 1969

Kechki Bungalow, Palamau: *Aranyer Dinratri*, 1969

Kechki Bungalow, Palamau: *Aranyer Dinratri*, 1969

After working on two consecutive films, I began to feel that the imperceptible wall between Manik-da and me was gradually disappearing. Soon after, he decided to make a film based on the novel *Pratidwandi*, and started discussing various aspects of photography with me. I was even allowed the privilege of attending meetings of his core unit members where they discussed the logistics of filming.

During this period, I accompanied him on recces on a regular basis, scouting for locations to shoot. In fact, wherever he went, I went. In other words, I started following him like his shadow. I was crazy about capturing him in my camera every moment.

Earlier, during the filming of *Goopy Gyne* and *Aranyer Dinratri*, I was in a way like a student standing outside the classroom – not being allowed entry. But now, Manik-da's body language hinted to me that it was no longer the case. I realized that

I had been able to attract the teacher's attention, and it is he who ushered me into the classroom holding me by the hand.

This inspired me more than ever. Perhaps it was this inspiration that helped me overcome that difficult phase, with only my old camera to aid me.

Pratidwandi is now history. The details of its picturization, using the city of Kolkata as the background – all these are now known to all. I shall, therefore, allude to another incident.

One day, a particular scene was being shot with Dhritiman standing at a specific location near the Tiger Cinema (which has now closed down) and the Manohar Das tank. After the shot was canned, Manik-da said, 'No, it won't do. Get some hippies.'

Just a while earlier, a few foreigners were roaming around that area. Manik-da sent Tinu (Anand) and me to go and find them. We roamed

New Market, Kolkata: *Pratidwandi*, February 1970

Chittaranjan Avenue, Kolkata: *Pratidwandi*, February 1970

Darjeeling: *Pratidwandi*, 1970

Kanthi, Medinipur: *Pratidwandi*, 1970

Digha, Medinipur: *Pratidwandi*, 1970

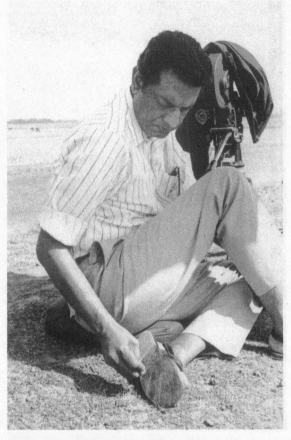

Digha, Medinipur: *Pratidwandi*, 1970

around the lanes and by-lanes and finally in utter desperation started raiding the hotels on Sudder Street. Ultimately, we found them in one such hotel. On explaining, they agreed to come with us. Manik-da was very pleased.

As on earlier occasions, I took a lot of photographs and as usual, Manik-da ticked those he liked and explained the shortcomings in the rest.

It was now that I came to be noticed by the public. People started realizing that I had taken some really good photographs. I started being approached for prints and negatives. Even professional photographers wanted to buy my negatives at rupees five apiece!

In fact, even at this point, I was unsure whether I would really be a full-fledged photographer. Not knowing what to do, I approached Manik-da one day and explained my predicament. Manik-da advised me not to give away negatives lest I be left with precious little.

Later, before the release of the film, Manik-da asked me for the negatives of a few of his selected stills for publicity. And it was for the first time that I had my name on the title card of a Satyajit Ray film.

At around this time, I received a call from another famous director to be the stills photographer of his forthcoming film. It was to be a professional contract. But at the very outset, I made it clear to the director that he would have to relieve me if ever there was any shooting by Manik-da during the duration of the contract. And he agreed. In fact, once, he allowed me to leave for Manik-da's outdoor shoot, when his own was on the floors. He was aware of my fascination for Manik-da. He also knew I would leave his job if he did not release me, irrespective of the loss I might suffer. My fascination for Manik-da was like that – unbridled, unreasonable.

Race Course, Kolkata: *Seemabaddha*, 1971

Indrapuri Studio, Kolkata: *Seemabaddha*, 1971

Race Course, Kolkata: *Seemabaddha*, 1971

Patna: *Seemabaddha*, 1971

After *Pratidwandi*, Manik-da turned his attention to *Seemabaddha*. One particular incident during the making of this film gave me immense satisfaction. It was necessary for this film to take a shot of Tata Centre from a house on Ballygunj Circular Road.

Relying on my ability, Manik-da explained to me how to take the shot. I took the photograph from a particular floor of Tivoli Court. Later, Manik-da took a six-foot print of it and used it on the sets for indoor shooting.

In spite of my increasing proximity to Manik-da, I could not quite shake off a feeling of uncertainty about him. Primarily, it was because of my inability to gauge whether the work was to his liking, as he was rarely vocal about his thoughts. At the same time, he would painstakingly guide me in my work. It was also as if he was the sole driving force and made me into a tireless worker, working against all odds, at all times – even today.

I learned one day that Manik-da was to shoot a documentary on Sikkim at the invitation of the Queen of Sikkim. Prior to this, I had no idea about documentary films. Naturally, I was also unsure about my responsibilities in such a venture. I was pleasantly surprised, however, to see my name as one among the listed eight-member team.

The primary theme of the film was the natural beauty of Sikkim. It was planned that the shooting would take place in three phases. We reached Sikkim in a few days' time. Initially, I was not quite clear about my role but within a few days I understood what was expected of me.

I started taking photographs of people, of locations and of handicrafts. Needless to say, I was also clicking Manik-da at work. We traversed the entire length and breadth of Sikkim, shooting at various places – from schools to slums to palaces – nothing was left uncaptured on camera.

One night in a guesthouse, seven of us were given two rooms to stay. One room was set aside

44

Gangtok, Sikkim: 1969

for Manik-da, while all of us accommodated ourselves in the other. But it was so crowded that I was coaxed into going to Manik-da's room.

It was a memorable night for me. Scared that I would start snoring once asleep or that my movements would disturb him, I stayed awake the entire night.

When I learnt of the expected date of the unit's return to Kolkata after the shoot, I was at my wits' end. The unit was scheduled to return to Kolkata two days after the performance of the play *Thug*. I had already given my word to the troupe. I had to reach Kolkata before the show, come what may.

But I was unable to gather the courage to go tell Manik-da about it. Ultimately, the production controller informed him of my predicament. Without a second thought, Manik-da arranged for my return.

If all this wasn't bad enough, my flight got delayed due to foggy weather. The show was at seven in the evening. I landed at the airport at six-thirty and rushed straight to Muktangan Theatre. I managed to do my part.

At this point, I came to the realization that it was time for me to choose between theatre and photography. To make both ends meet it was essential to have a full-time job. Over and above that it was impossible to spare time for both ventures simultaneously.

But both theatre and photography were equally dear to me. It was difficult for me to choose, to give up either. After much soul searching, I discovered I was leaning towards photography. Perhaps Manik-da's irresistible charisma pushed me to take this decision.

Whatever my achievements in the field of photography, even to this day I am unable to forget theatre – my first love. That is why whenever a new play is performed anywhere, I try to capture the moments in my camera. Even though I haven't acted in a play in a long time, I maintain my link with theatre through the camera.

Paus Mela, Santiniketan: *The Inner Eye*, 1972

Kalabhavan Chhatranivas, Santiniketan: *The Inner Eye,* 1972

Kalabhavan, Santiniketan: *The Inner Eye*, 1972

Kathmandu, Nepal: *The Inner Eye*, 1972

Manik-da wanted to do a documentary called *The Inner Eye*, on his teacher at Santiniketan, Benodebehari Mukhopadhyay, the revered artist. For it, he decided to travel to many places across north India in search of the source of inspiration of Benodebehari. I, too, came to be part of his group.

Travelling by air, staying in five-star hotels – it was all very new to me. We went to Nepal via Rajasthan, Delhi and Varanasi. I took a lot of photographs of Manik-da and earned a lot of praise from many people for them.

Ashani Sanket is a film worth mentioning for more than one reason. Firstly, it was Manik-da's second film in colour. Also, Manik-da was once again adapting a Bibhutibhushan Bandyopadhyay novel, after the Apu trilogy.

The film was shot mostly in Birbhum. A house

was constructed along the road. Manik-da decided the positioning of each and every object – from the cage of the parrot to the bamboo bridge, and even the bottle gourd creeper. A test shooting was also conducted with Soumitra-da (Chattopadhyay). I have those pictures captured in my camera as well.

The film was shot over a period of one year, in order to capture the diversity of the seasons. Before the film was released, Manik-da asked me for a few still shots for publicity. The tag of 'amateur photographer' pinched me because all the technicians used to get paid and I was the lone exception. I would often wonder: doesn't my work, all my labour, have any value?

When Manik-da asked for the negatives of the *Asbani Sanket* stills, I was desperate and ready to literally beg with my palm outstretched before him. One day, in front of his producer and production controller I said, 'Please give me at least a rupee. I just want to be a professional.' I was beginning to regret it even as the words tumbled out of my mouth. I wondered how Manik-da would take it.

He was silent for a while and then said, 'Why just one rupee? Your work is worth much more than that.' Hearing him say those words at that time gave me a lot of encouragement, and they continue to inspire me even now.

How Babita came to be part of *Ashani Sanket* is an interesting story in itself. Just after the 1971 war, I was on a mission to take photographs of cine stars in Bangladesh for the journal *Cine Advance*. The Bangladeshi actress Suchanda told me, 'Dada, I don't aspire for much more. Rather you take a photograph of my sister and show it to Manik-da.' I agreed. The shoot was scheduled at actor Razzak's house. When I saw the girl come out with make-up on her face, I got her to wash her face clean and took her photograph. That girl was no one else but Babita. Manik-da was then contemplating a film on a Buddhadeb Basu story 'Ekti Jibon'. I approached him to give Babita a role, but he said he had already decided on another girl to play the character. Of course, that film never materialized for many reasons.

Bolpur: *Ashani Sanket*, 1972

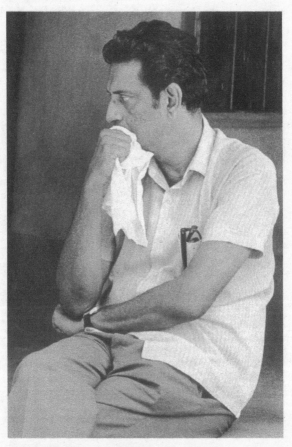

Dangapara, Bolpur: *Ashani Sanket*, 1972

Dangapara, Bolpur: *Ashani Sanket*, 1972

Dangapara, Bolpur: *Ashani Sanket*, 1972

Dangapara, Bolpur: *Ashani Sanket*, 1972

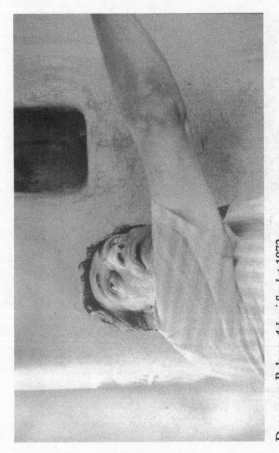

Dangapara, Bolpur. *Ashani Sanket*, 1972

Some time later, while Manik-da was looking at my photographs, he suddenly tapped at the picture of Babita and said, 'Why not *Ashani Sanket*?'

Thereafter, Babita came to Kolkata and appeared for a screen test. The rest is history.

Sonar Kella was based on a story written by Manik-da himself. This was the first time that Phelu-da, the favourite detective of all Bengalis, would be seen on the silver screen. We were to proceed to Delhi. The day before the departure, out of sheer excitement, I bought a new camera – Canon FTB.

From Delhi we went to Rajasthan. The film was shot all over the state – Jaipur, Jodhpur, Jaisalmer and Bikaner. I clicked to my heart's content. I thought quite a few of them were good. On my return to Kolkata, I sent the rolls to be developed. But all my hard work was undone by a stroke of bad luck – some chink in the camera had caused light to enter and had subsequently spoiled the film. I was utterly disappointed.

So dejected was I, that I could not even face Manik-da. Sandip, Manik-da's son, came to know about it and passed the information of my debacle on to Manik-da. A few days later, Manik-da himself rang me up, and in an unusually soft tone told me, 'Let bygones be bygones. Come on, let us all join hands and see what can be done. Don't worry.' His kind voice and the use of the word 'us' made me weep. All my grief over the loss of the photographs got washed away in those tears. Later, Manik-da marked the portions in those photographs that had been affected by light and framed them.

This was Manik-da. He had that unusual quality of leadership. During location shootings, if the call time was at six in the morning, he would be ready by five-thirty and silently walk up and down the verandah outside our room.

Perhaps only a great artist can appreciate other artists and the art that lives in their soul. One evening during the shooting of *Sonar Kella*, we were all engrossed in the music played by a native musician. Our production controller gave him a hundred-rupee note but Manik-da asked him to

Indrapuri Studio, Kolkata: *Sonar Kella*, January 1974

NEMAI GHOSH

pay the man five hundred rupees. He had such
deep regard for an artist.

I even had a small role in *Sonar Kella*. I was given
a one-page script. Manik-da told me I would have
to do in front of the camera all that I had been
doing, for so long, behind it. My role was that of
a photographer. I was to take some photographs
of Mukul.

Manik-da's first Hindi film was based on *Shatranj
Ke Khiladi*, a famous story by Munshi Premchand.
It was to be shot in colour. The cast was full of
famous actors and actresses. I, however, was not
to be part of the film as the producer had arranged
for a photographer from Mumbai for the stills.
When Manik-da came to know, he said, 'Let them
do whatever they like. But only Nemai will take my
stills.' Ultimately, of course, the photographer from
Mumbai could not keep pace with Manik-da and
left within a week. So I was left to do the job myself.
Manik-da got a few of the colour transparencies of

Victoria Memorial Hall, Kolkata: *Shatranj Ke Khiladi*, 1977

Victoria Memorial Hall, Kolkata: *Shatranj Ke Khiladi*, 1977

Deorai Kalan, Lucknow: *Shatranj Ke Khiladi*, 1977

this film processed from abroad. Those days such processing could not be done here properly. For the purposes of the lobby cards, I unhesitatingly gave away many of the transparencies to the producer. In return, I received only one set of the lobby stills.

Sadgati was a telefilm made for Doordarshan, based on, again, a Munshi Premchand story. It was shot in Chhattisgarh – then part of Madhya Pradesh. One day, while shooting with Gita Siddharth and Mohan Agashe, Manik-da suddenly saw dark clouds in the sky and asked Smita (Patil) and Om Puri to quickly get ready. He advised the technicians to prepare to shoot another scene. But before they could arrange the paraphernalia, the clouds erupted. It began pouring heavily and in that incessant rain, right in front of my eyes, the memorable scene was shot. In fact, Manik-da's very presence, the manner in which he instructed the unit, created such magic. All of a sudden, even in the fading light of the evening sky, amidst pouring rain, everyone went on working. The result is now history—one of the most remarkable sequences in Manik-da's films. But there is something that remains a secret to all. Let me share it here.

I have quite a few very personal photographs of Manik-da – not to be shared with anybody. These were only for me. In that special collection of mine, another photograph was added that day: Manik-da running around in a *fatua* (half-kurta), holding his dhoti in one hand in a futile effort to save it from the mud and water.

Jai Baba Phelunath was the second film in the Phelu-da series. After its completion, we all went to Rajasthan for *Hirak Rajar Deshe*. Babu (Sandip Ray) also did some photography with me on this trip. But back in Kolkata, I found that not a single shot had come out properly. Babu too suffered the same fate. It was such a disappointment for us both. So many unusual moments lost, never to return again.

Manik-da, however, was not unduly concerned about this and asked us to prepare well for the second phase of shooting. We realized later that sudden changes in temperature made our cameras malfunction.

Varanasi: *Jai Baba Phelunath*, February 1978

Varanasi: *Jai Baba Phelunath*, February 1978

Varanasi: *Jai Baba Phelunath*, February 1978

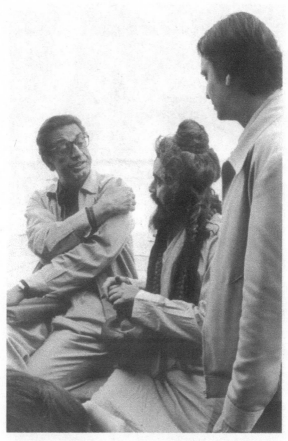

Dwarbhanga Ghat, Varanasi: *Jai Baba Phelunath*, February 1978

Purulia: *Hirak Rajar Deshe*, October 1980

The locations for *Hirak Rajar Deshe* required a forest. It was therefore decided that Manik-da would spend a day inspecting some forests in north Bengal. I would accompany him.

Alighting at Siliguri, we found the forest officer waiting for us with a convoy. He was our guide on the trip. Without wasting even a moment, Manik-da got down to work. Almost spellbound, I studied him. This man, who had been so widely recognized with all sorts of awards, was inspecting one forest after another, in search of a perfect spot for the shot, keeping in mind the requirements of easy mobility of the entire group and of vehicles, safe preservation of cameras and other equipment and above all, accommodation for the artists and technicians.

After a day's wandering, we put up at a nearby forest bungalow for the night. We were to resume our search the following morning. I decided to wake up before dawn. However, much before

dawn I was woken up by a deep-throated voice:
'Nemai, Nemai'. Manik-da was up and ready and
standing near the head of my bedstead. That's
when I realized, try as hard as I may, I could follow
him, but never *be* him. It was beyond me to reach
anywhere close to his willpower or speed.

Manik-da was doing the film *Piku* for a French
producer. I was unaware, but somehow, I reached
the location. I ended up taking a few very candid
photographs of Manik-da at work during this
shoot.

Rabindranath Tagore's *Ghare Baire* is one of my
favourite novels. Manik-da had been planning to
adapt it for long, but for many reasons it was not
materializing.

In fact, he had already sketched all the
characters. He was looking for a new face for the
role of Bimala. Once, around that time, I remember
boarding a tramcar from Park Circus, thinking
about the story, contemplating the sketches that

Manik-da had made. In the pensive mood, the first thing I saw was 'Bimala' sitting in the ladies' seat. I could not gather the courage to approach her and put forward the proposal for acting in a film in front of so many passengers. So I just kept an eye on her. The tram ride went on. Finally, she alighted at Dharmatala. I also got down, followed and caught up with her in front of Jyoti Cinema, and apprised her of my proposal. I gave her my card and Manik-da's phone number, went straight to Manik-da and told him everything. A week passed and still no call. Manik-da was worried and said, 'The lady is still not contacting us. Why did you not take her address?'

A few days later, when I was showing Manik-da photographs of some stage performances shot by me, a face caught his attention. He asked for an enlarged print of the same. He then saw the play live and asked me to get in touch with the actress – Swatilekha. She did not respond immediately but later consented. This was how Manik-da did everything, every choice was spot on, flawless, well thought out and well merited.

Once, a fair, young boy came to see him and expressed his desire to act in his film. Manik-da did not entertain him. But, for his next film he suddenly remembered the boy for the hero's role. He did not even remember his name. He gave me a description of the boy and asked me to try and locate him. He also said the boy was acting in the play *Lambakarna*.

Manik-da knew I was fond of drama. Moreover, I had not seen the play as yet. I contacted Shyamal Ghosh of the Nakshatra drama group. During rehearsals, Shyamal told his troupe that Manik-da was looking for the boy who had been to his house. Two days later, two boys met me and I sent them to Manik-da. Unfortunately, neither of them was the face Manik-da was looking for. A few days later, when I went to meet him, I saw a boy at Manik-da's house. He said, 'This is the boy I was looking for!' The boy was Pradip Mukherjee, the hero of *Jana Aranya*.

Kolkata: *Jana Aranya*, 1975

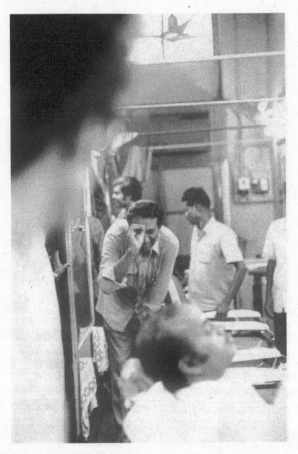

A.N. John, Park Street, Kolkata: *Jana Aranya*, 1975

Flurys, Park Street, Kolkata: *Jana Aranya*, 1975

Indrapuri Studio, Kolkata: *Jana Aranya*, 1975

Maidan, Kolkata: *Jana Aranya*, 1975

Maidan, Kolkata: *Jana Aranya*, 1975

During the shooting of *Ghare Baire*, I saw a picture book on Hitchcock at work. I thought perhaps a similar book could be produced with Manik-da's photographs too. That is, if I could capture every moment of his making of *Ghare Baire* – perhaps bring to light the continuity of my photographs in the form of a book, as an alternative commentary.

We were shooting on the film in Barddhaman. After a shot was taken, something crossed Manik-da's mind. He stopped shooting and seemed to be engrossed in some thought. Maybe he was thinking of how to improve the shot. The outdoor location was teeming with people. I thought he was perhaps looking for some solitude. And so it was. I saw Manik-da make his way through the crowd. I followed him. Roy-da (Soumendu Roy) asked me not to. Without paying heed to his advice, I continued to follow Manik-da, albeit from a safe distance. I saw him take a few long strides and sit by a pond, his chin cupped in his palm, a group of young boys shouting around him. But in such deep contemplation was he that nothing seemed to disturb him. He appeared like a rishi in a state of peaceful meditation. I captured this moment on camera.

Manik-da had his first heart attack during the shooting of *Ghare Baire*. Excess workload and the many uncertainties of film-making against all odds seemed to have taken a toll of his health. Doctors advised him to take complete rest.

And so he did. Suddenly one day, he said he wanted to shoot the last scene of *Ghare Baire* himself. All the arrangements were made in a hurry. I was given the responsibility of escorting him safely to the shooting spot in Barddhaman. That was one of the toughest moments of my life.

On the way, Manik-da wanted to have a cup of tea at a roadside dhaba. I arranged for an earthen cup of tea for him. Ultimately, I escorted him safely to Barddhaman and breathed a sigh of relief.

A feeling of great sorrow overwhelmed me as we made our way to the location. Manik-da had been an almost godlike personality to me – my inspiration, the source of my strength. Many a time in the past had I faltered trying to keep pace with him – and today I was having to escort him like this!

For me, *Ghare Baire* was a memorable film for an entirely different reason. After that incident of me asking for a fee of a rupee so that I might be considered a professional – during *Ashani Sanket* – this was the first time the production controller told me I would get a fee of Rs 7,500 for this film. I was delighted. Though in the mean time I had worked as a professional photographer in many other films, being a professional in Manik-da's film was an entirely different matter.

Manik-da grew very weak after this attack. He used to lament about his health before Dr Bakshi. I remember Dr Bakshi being very enthusiastic about my photography. Even as Manik-da went through a long period of recovery, I would click his photographs whenever he looked a bit fresh. Dr Bakshi would show him the photographs and say, 'Come now! You don't look ill at all!' Manik-da felt happy seeing those photographs. That was the greatest gift to me.

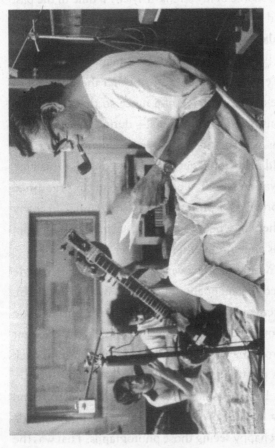

HMV Recording Studio, Dumdum, Kolkata: *Ghare Baire*, 1983

Barddhaman: *Gbare Baire*, March 1983

Barddhaman: *Ghare Baire*, March 1983

At times, I used to feel greatly disturbed – as if his illness rendered me an orphan. I did not know what to do. I used to go to his house but could not enter his room as freely as I was accustomed to earlier. I would just peep in and enter only when he called me.

This was the time someone, whom I do not want to name, tried to create a rift between Manik-da and me. But try as much as he did, he could not succeed because of the affection and love I enjoyed from Boudi (Mrs Ray) and Babu.

One day a girl called Runki (Banerjee) came to see me. She introduced herself as the young Durga of *Pather Panchali*. She was at the time associated with a publishing house. And she had come to meet me as a representative of her organization.

She studied my collection of photographs at length. Excitedly she asked me, 'What have you done! You keep so many photographs lying like this! Please do something. If nothing else, at least publish a book.'

With great conviction and enthusiasm she told me that if a book with these photographs could ever be published, it would give future generations invaluable insights into the life and times of India's greatest film-maker. It would be a collector's edition.

I was taken aback. For the last few years I had been looking at Manik-da and the world of his cinema through my lens only as an attentive student. I had taken lots of photographs, but never even for a moment did I think what could be done with them. I had only worked like one possessed.

I also had a passion for writing. I had written a report on the shooting of *Pratidwandi*. I used to keep notes of my experiences. Once, an essay of mine was published in a journal titled *Continental Film Review*. Manik-da liked it.

Soon after, I wrote another essay and showed it to Manik-da. He kept it with him. When he returned it to me, I found it totally different from my original. He had polished and elevated it to a wonderful write-up. I did not have the audacity to

publish Manik-da's writing as mine. So, to this day
I retain that essay with me.

Afterwards, a publishing house in Kolkata proposed
that I write a book with Manik-da's photographs.
An attractive proposition! I went to show the draft
contract to Manik-da.

Usually, whenever I was apprehensive of asking
something of him, I used to take the help of Boudi.
This time too, I told Boudi about it. She took
me to Manik-da and said, 'Look, Nemai is going
to write a book. He wants to talk to you about
royalty.' Manik-da was busy doing something. He
just raised his eyes and looked at us. He heard the
details of the proposal and said, 'Nemai will write
a book and for that I shall have to take money!
Never, I will never take any money from him!'

The gentleman I referred to earlier – whose
name I refrained from mentioning – told me
jokingly that because I did not do the photography
for *Pather Panchali*, my book would be incomplete

and, in fact, worthless. But how could I be blamed for that? And why did not those who were there at the time carefully preserve their work if they had systematically done the photography? All this just motivated me and I decided I must do the book at any cost.

I selected some pictures, arranged them in several albums and showed them to Manik-da. Surprised at the volume of the collection, he said, 'When did you take so many photographs?'

But as luck would have it, the Kolkata-based organization ultimately backed out. Though disheartened, I continued my effort. Eventually, quite a few publishers from Delhi showed interest. But the trouble there was some of them wanted a recommendation letter from some political bigwig. Others asked for a write-up by Manik-da of around twenty pages.

At around this time, Ravi Sabarwal of Time Books advised me to contact some overseas publishers.

I used to occasionally discuss the theme of the proposed book with Babu. This was when I thought that if ever I could get my book published, the Foreword would be by the one whom I had from a distance, like Ekalavya, regarded as my guru in photography. He is none other than Henri Cartier-Bresson.

I started writing letters to Cartier-Bresson without telling anyone. Initially, he showed no interest. After about a year of correspondence, he agreed to just see my photographs. He asked me to meet him in Paris with the photographs – from Kalighat, Kolkata, straight to Rivoli, Paris.

Manik-da was stunned when he learnt all this. Perhaps he was a little wary of my crazy endeavour. But he did not say anything. In fact, my relationship with Manik-da was based on mutual trust – complete and total faith. He would understand me, even without words being spoken.

When I had planned the meeting with Cartier-Bresson, Sandip said he would join me if I postponed the programme by about a month. So I fixed a fresh date of appointment after a month. However, due to unforeseen circumstances, Sandip got stuck at London and I was left to tread forth alone.

Perhaps at another time I will write about my experience of locating Bresson's house, traversing the streets of Paris in a taxi, enjoying their hospitality, and having to stay in an expensive hotel. Suffice it to say that both Bresson and his wife were overjoyed at seeing my photographs. Not only did I get a Foreword from my photography guru, but also an invitation to breakfast with him and a local publisher next morning. The icing on the cake came when the publisher showed eagerness to publish my book.

Still, for whatever reason, the publication kept getting delayed. I was anxious because I wanted to get the book out before Manik-da's seventieth birthday. Just at that time, my friend Andrew Robinson proposed to publish a book with seventy of my photographs.

He asked an organization in Brussels to do the job. But they said that if I could not reach Brussels in time with 200 negatives, they would be unable to go ahead, as they had to simultaneously keep pace with their commitments for the Cannes Film Festival. So I went there and in consultation with them selected seventy of the 200 negatives.

I did not mention this to anybody as I wanted to surprise Manik-da. It would be my offering to him, to my inspiration.

Ultimately, the book came out in August 1991. With the first copy in my hand I ran to Bishop Lefroy Road, to Manik-da's house. I presented him the copy and offered my pranams by touching his feet. He immediately stood up and embraced me. I knew, however much one tried, one would never succeed in creating a rift between us.

Manik-da never showed any pride. He did not have the slightest vanity. He had the simplicity of a child. He believed in doing his work himself. For any requirement he would make the phone call himself. He would receive all phone calls himself. He would open the door himself, attend to his guests and see them off at the door personally.

Once, he rang me up for a negative. I was not home at the time and returned rather late after a night show. I thought of ringing him up early next morning. But late at night, I received another phone call from him. Manik-da said he was expecting my call.

On another occasion, not being able to get me on the phone when he needed me, he simply drove down to my house. To him there was no one superior or inferior, high or low. He believed in giving everyone their due regard.

Whenever I would go to his place, I would always find him engrossed in something or other. He used to effortlessly sketch or draw pictures, or do calligraphy. Once complete, he never cared much to preserve his works. He was interested only in creation.

I told him once that I wanted to keep a copy of his different types of works. Manik-da readily agreed. I requested him to sketch the screenplay of a film in a particular colour so that it might be easier for me to copy it later when needed. Manik-da obliged me again.

Such was the greatness of the man.

My son Satyaki is now a professional photographer. He was just out of college when I took him to the National Library for some work with Manik-da. From a pile of old newspapers, Manik-da dug out his work to show him.

I got Satyaki to make the copies and told Manik-da that his copies were as good as my own. When Manik-da saw those prints later, he said, 'Nemai, one more photographer has now joined your family.' As a father, these words gave me immense joy.

During my absence, Manik-da got Satyaki to do his work. In fact age, race, religion – none of these ever mattered to him. He was ever-encouraging. It was primarily because of his inspiration that I could restore some of his invaluable creations outside the film world. Really, I could never imagine even in my wildest dream that someone like me could ever get so much of support from such a towering talent.

On another occasion an incident took place which made me realize the depth of my relationship with Manik-da. He had asked me my plans for the following day. I told him that I was doing nothing in particular. He then asked me to meet him at his house with my camera.

Without realizing what was in store, I reached his house with my camera rather excited. Both of us got into his car. I still had no idea where we were going. Suddenly, I realized we were in front of Ballygunj Government School.

It was Manik-da's school. While entering the school premises, for the first time in my life I saw Manik-da get emotional. From there we went to Garpar, his ancestral house. But unfortunately the house was locked. So I could not take a photograph of the room where Manik-da had opened his eyes to the world.

I had travelled a lot with Manik-da. But getting a peek into his past that day drew me closer to him. At least for that one day he was not the famous director Satyajit Ray. He was just a man who was reminiscing about his past and returning to the memories of his childhood. And I was the lone witness.

Manik-da could complete in his lifetime all the work he initiated after *Ghare Baire*. I was associated with all the work from *Ganashatru* to *Agantuk*. While shooting the documentary on Sukumar Ray, my son also joined me in.

This documentary was a marvellous project. In fact, Sukumar Ray was perhaps the only one in his league.

Running parallel with these wonderful memories are a few dark ones. It is better not to allude to those in the context of such a great personality. Towards the final stages, things had come to such a pass that I often felt like quitting. I struggled but decided to continue, lest my absence upset Manik-da. He remained the same to me till the end. Sandip, Boudi or other members of the household also remained the same. My gratitude towards them knows no end.

Indrapuri Studio, Kolkata: *Agantuk*, November 1990

Sukna, Siliguri: *Shakha Prashakha*, January 1990

Goalpara, Santiniketan: *Agantuk*, January 1991

Two days in the year have been very special to me – Manik-da's birthday and his marriage anniversary. On these occasions I would visit him early in the morning. And on the day of the anniversary, I would jokingly tell him that I was his director for the day. I would even suggest to Boudi the previous evening which saree she should wear on the occasion.

They would pose the way I instructed. I have many intimate photographs of them. Manik-da would often tease me and say, 'Look! Don't get these published ever.'

Boudi was literally his better half. Once, on his birthday, I thought of not attending the evening function as I was nursing a fractured arm. But I had to agree to go on Boudi's insistence. Boudi fed me with her own hands.

All these memories keep me alive today, inspire me to work. I know not whether I deserve what I received. I can only say that my inspiration, my experiences were but small pebbles that I picked up from the shores of a mighty ocean called Satyajit Ray.

Manik-da's death remains perhaps the most devastating incident in my life. It brought to an end a chapter in my life. I had spent the best years of my life in his company. The man lives in my mind. I was shattered when I learnt he was no more. I had never dreamt of a situation where Manik-da would leave me. Even now I cannot.

I was at his doorstep on the last day. Embracing his motionless body, Boudi was weeping – Sandip too. I do not need a photograph to remind me of that moment. Even today I can see the picture clearly in my mind's eye.

Standing in the sun you are sure to shine in its light. Such was Manik-da's presence in my life. A mere touch of his created this photographer Nemai Ghosh out of a common boy from a middle-class family.

I was fortunate to have met him. From that moment onwards, for twenty-five long years I have been sheltered under this huge tree. My sincerity, my struggle for perfection are all thanks to the example set by him. Even to this day, whenever I am alone at home, I reminisce all those golden moments. He is no more; his memory, his photographs are what keep me going, give me inspiration for new ventures. Those memories, incidents – big and small – energize me, are my raison d'etre. I have learnt the lessons of life from him. Like him, I want to continue to work till my last breath. This is my only prayer, my only desire.